Autana

Eye of the Gods

Stephen Platt

www.leveretpublishing.com

Autana: Eye of the Gods
Second Edition - July 2017
Published by
Leveret Publishing
56 Covent Garden, Cambridge, CB1 2HR, UK

ISBN 978-1-9124600-1-4

© Stephen Platt 2015

All rights reserved. No part of this publication may be reproduced, stored in a retrieval system or transmitted in any form by any means, electronic, mechanical, photocopying, recording or otherwise, except brief extracts for the purpose of review, without the written permission of the publisher.

Autana

Cerro Autana, a small isolated tepui, or table mountain composed of Lower Precambrian sandstones and quartzites of the ancient Venezuelan Guiana Shield.

Autana 1974

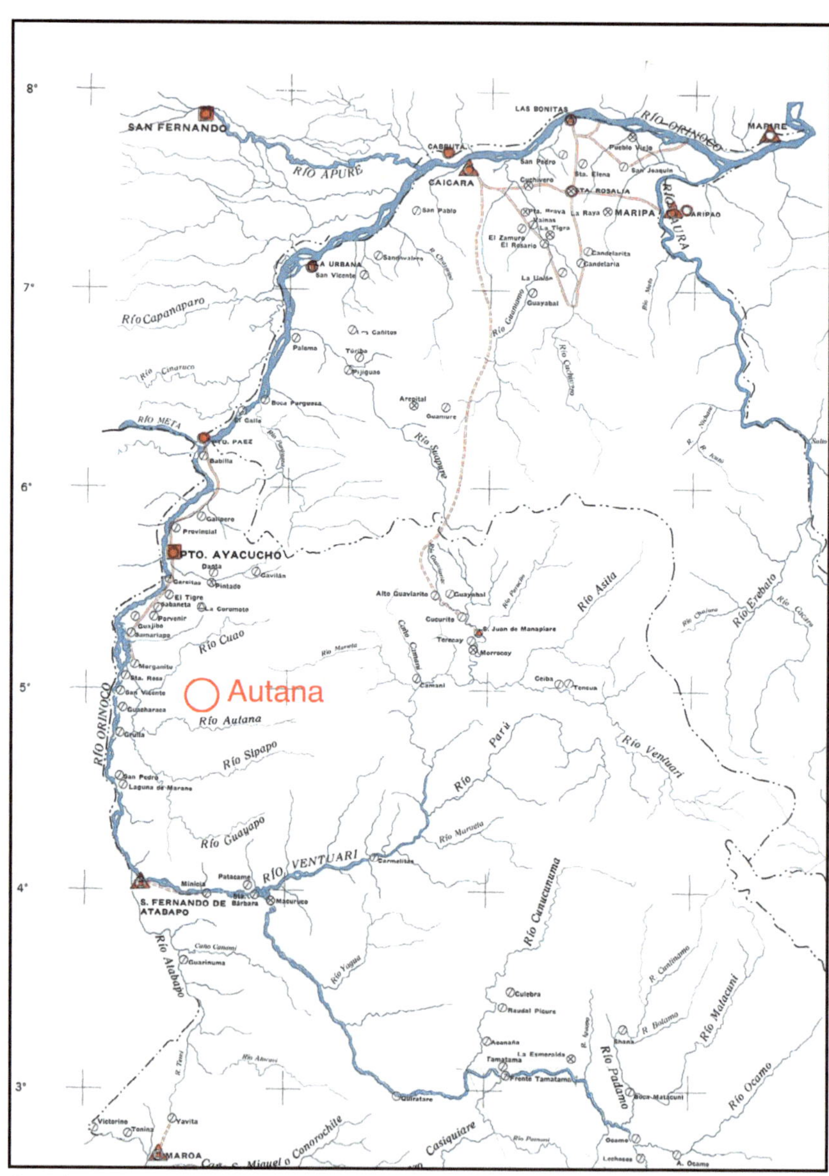

Cerro Autana – south of Puerto Ayacucho, Gran Sabana, Federal Amazonas, Venezuela

Introduction

El Autana is a sandstone tepuy or butte about 400 miles south of Caracas in the Amazon Territory of Venezuela. We climbed the north ridge in 1974.

A cathedral sized cave pierces the mountain from side to side, so that light shines through about 400 ft from the top. Like all good jungle mountains, this too has its Indian legend. At dusk, when the sun shines through the cave that pierces the mountain from one side to side, the Piaroa Indians call the cave the 'Eye of the Gods'.

Stephen Platt, David Nott, Wilmer Perez la Riva and Carlos Reyes climbed the North Ridge in its entirety in three days and then descended to the caves were we spent a further three nights, exploring the galleries and traversing around the mountain along the horizontal fault line at the height of the cave.

On the final day we completed the ridge to the summit but night caught us abseiling down the last overhanging 300ft wall and we stumbled back to base camp by the meagre light of our only pocket torch.

Cerro Autana view from the north. 4°52' north and 67°27'. Altitude 1,300m, walls 900m

About the Autana

Cerro Autana is known as Wahari-Kuawi which means *'sacred tree of the fruits of the world'*. The Piaroa, the indigenous people who live in this region, believe that the Autana is the surviving stump of this enormous tree.

It is situated 4°52' north and 67°27' west in an area of forested savannah bounded by the rivers Autana and Cuao, tributaries of the River Sipapo which flows into the Orinoco up stream from the Maipures rapids. It is about 100km south of Puerto Ayacucho, capital of the Amazon Territory of Venezuela.

It is predominately red in colour and belongs to the series known as Roraima. It measures just over 2km north to south and 400 metres east to west. It is in two parts. A tower rising to 1,300 metres, with a lower tail stretching off to the south. The tower is a monolith of quartz and red sandstone with near vertical walls of up to 900 metres.

A deep fault divides the main body of the tower from a buttress to the north which forms the North Ridge, the route of our ascent. Charles

View from the east showing caves and line of our ascent up right-hand ridge

Brewer Carias, David Nott and Robert Madden, a photographer from the National Geopgraphic, descended this chasm, having landed on the summit by helicopter, and were the first to explore the caves in September 1971.

The first ascent of the Autana was in 1974 by two Englishmen, Stephen Platt, David Nott, and two Venezuelans, Wilmer Perez la Riva and Carlos Reyes. They climbed the North Ridge in its entirety and then descended to the caves. They climbed back up the Brewer-Nott chasm and then abseiled back down the whole route.

The dome of the main cavern is about 40 metres above the cave floor. The 'sacrificial stone' in the mouth of this cave measures 4.5 metres by 1-1.5 metres. In all there are 12 openings in the cave system, one of which pierces the mountain from one side to the other.

View from the north showing and line of our ascent up the north ridge

Getting to the Autana

We needed to take outboard motors and petrol for the curiara we would use to ascend the Orinoco from Puerto Ayacucho.

From Caracas we drove in two vehicles, first west towards Maracay and south at La Encrucijada to San Fernando de Apure via Cagua and Villa de Cura. This was familiar territory from climbing trips to the limestone pillars at San Juan de los Moros. The paved road ended after we had crossed the mighty Apure River and since the rainy season had only just ended there was plenty of mud and we got stuck and had to haul each other out numerous times.

From San Fernando de Apure we crossed the Arauco, Cunaviche, Campanaparo and Cinaruco on oil drum rafts because back then there were no bridges and finally got to Puerto Paez on the Orinoco and crossed by large chalana. To avoid the Atures rapids one drives south through Puerto Ayacucho to Samariapo where we left the drums of gasoline for our expedition to the Autana later in the year.

The following day we boarded a large bongo with a roof we could sling hammocks under and travelled south on the Orinoco, past its confluence

River crossing in Steve's long wheel base Land Rover full of outboard motors

with the Rio Ventuari at Santa Barbara and on past Tamatama, where the black waters of the Rio Negro enter the of the Orinoco via the natural Casiquiare Canal that joins the Orinoco to the Amazon. On past the mission at La Esmeralda, to the mouth of the Ocamo where we swopped vessel for a narrow curiara. On past the Mavaca and Manaviche the river narrows and the rapids begin and we had to climb out numerous times to manhandle the dugout off rocks. On as far as Platanal, near the headwaters of the Orinoco, to collect the French anthropologist Jacques Lizot..

Car ferry chalana crossing Orinocco at Puerto Paez

Scenes from the Llanos and Orinoco

The Eye of the Gods

Extract from Journal of the Cambridge University Mountaineering Club 1976

We were in a slender dugout canoe pottering up the Orinoco River bound for El Autana. Memories of the hassle at the airport in Maiquetia, when we arrived ten minutes before takeoff with outboard motor were dropping away. The three Makiritare Indians who would help us carry gear to the base snoozed in the prow. David Nott, Wilmur Perez, Carlos Reyes and I lay on the gear while Juan, a Piaroa Indian acted as cox.

Weeks before we had flown round the mountain and had picked out a route – the North Ridge – from the consistently vertical walls of the crag. This 2,000 ft ridge rises in a series of three steps, which we hoped would provide bivouac sites.

We drove 80km south from Puerto Ayacucho to reach the river port of Samariapo along the road that skirts the unnavegable Atures Rapids, which divide the Upper and Lower Orinoco. The next morning we boarded

David and Steve bathing in the Orinocco at Samariapo, where we boarded a curiara

Juan in the prow of the curiara chopping a way past fallen trees in Caño Manteco

the curiara, a large dugout canoe. We spent a leisurely day in the canoe and another humping bags to base camp. Here the Makiritare cleared an opening in the forest and built a massive frame support for hammocks and tarpaulin in little more time than it takes to put up a tent.

The base camp was still some way from the rock but was by the last stream, which we were glad of to wash off sweat and grime each night. We were we were taking things at a fairly leisurely place, still hoping Daniel Genoud would catch us up. Daniel worked for the Venezuelan Fontiers Commission

Juan paddling curiara up Caño Manteco

Steve's first attempt to get established on the ridge with Daniel Genoud

Steve taking higher line in, successful second attempt

and had organised the whole trip. Wilmer and I had been with him on various expeditions with him, including to the Serrania de Perijá, 'marking' the borders with Colombia and Brazil. But Daniel had, annoyingly, been sent to the Isla de los Roques by his boss Daniel Panchenco.

I lay in my hammock late as the others set off the first day. I had done the first couple of pitches on a previous reconnaissance trip with Daniel, but had failed to complete a steep traverse to get onto the ridge proper and hahd had to lower off.

Today, David led the two pitches to the start of the first steep section, an overhanging traverse onto a very steep committing ridge.

"The belay's not too brilliant", David said, throwing me the runners.

"All this effort to get here and now I don't fancy it," I thought.

Up a groove to an overhanging jamming crack and a lovely thread. A horizontal crack line ran right to the prow of the ridge and the safety of a waiting tree, but the intervening 30ft were very steep. A tentative step, with the left hand firmly jammed, and I began to swing off, pushed out by the bulging wall. My right hand was fiddling about, trying to find a finger hold,but found nothing and so I retreated. Finally, I managed to find a finger hold and launched off before I had time to regret it. There was very little for the hands and I had to keep moving to avoid falling off.

"My god, I should have pegged this", I thought. "I'll be penduluming about under the overhangs without prussiks in a minute!"

The holds gave out about five feet from the tree. I got a knee on the traverse line to hold myself in while I fumbled for a peg. I usually drop them at times like that but this one went in beautifully and after a welcome rest things suddenly went easily to the tree. There was no stance, so I moved on to the end of the rope, but still found no belay. The ridge above was steep and holdless and David wasn't enthusiastic about coming up to the tree. Nobody else seemed keen so, with a back rope around the tree, I pendulumed back to the ledge.

That night as I climbed into my hammock the prospects did not seem so good. The rock was steep and holdless and we had been easily defeated. Still, the next morning, David spotted a line some way to the left leading to a large solitary tree at the begiining of a possible traverse line. Two 150ft pitches of easy VS and four hours of sack hauling and we were there – only another nasty traverse under more overhangs to get back to the ridge. This time we had to reach the ridge, since the wall above overhung all the way to the cave.

David went up to the overhang and began to move right, got a peg in and

Penduluming back to ledge

used this to make a massive stride to a large foothold. There he stopped and finally came back down on a very small nut.

Tomorrow would be the big day, and we could no longer wait for Daniel as we had no more fixed ropes to leave for him.

I managed the stride next morning and after one or two nasty moves up found a hidden pocket hold. Another traverse and we were on the ridge. Wilmur came up to the belay and I had a look round the corner. The ridge was still steep but there was a good crack and more good pockets. The first 50ft were hard; I thought I was off once, but then the angle started to relent and I knew we had made it to the top of the first step.

We spent our first night in a bivouac dangling from pegs. The three others found room to sit hunched on a ledge but I found a narrow soil covered ledge and was able to stretch out in my sleeping bag. I awoke to the others laughing at me. The soil had slipped away in the night and I was dangling on the smooth near vertical slab, held on only by the two coils of rope I had wrapped round my body

David on upper pitches

Nearing the top

The second step was a series of delightful 70ft walls. The climbing was never desperate but exciting on the prow of the ridge. Our second bivouac was a superb grassy platform with views along both east and west walls. A big fire, plenty of food and a perfect sunset lit the distant river like a string of pearls.

Carlos had climbed the next big pitch and had left a rope for tomorrow. We had been watching him all afternoon, basking in the sunshine, as he inched his way up a chimney right in the middle of the ridge. I had planned to jumar up this, but the next day Carlos told me that this would not be fair, since he and Wilmur had been climbing all my leads.

Things went fairly easily at first and we began to think that we would reach the cave that day. But hours later we had still got a long traverse to do to the cave and only two hours of light. Halfway along this delicate traverse I pulled off a massive flake. There was a crashing of undergrowth and a few choice words but I was alright.

I moved up to a stance, belayed and took in the rope to find that it had chopped it in two. I descended the gully hoping to find the rest of the rope in one piece as we only had two ropes and we needed both of them for the

Entering the cave with the so called 'sacrificial' stone at its mouth. Formed 300 million years ago, these are amongst the oldest caves in the world. This the main cavern is 40metres high.

Abseiling into the caves

Carlos Reyes in the cathedral like cave

long abseils on the way back down. The rope was buried under lots of soil and in three bits, but still all there. I calmed down, tied it together and brought the others up.

The traverse line continued from here as a wide ledge and we were able to drag the sacks across. The ledge finally ran out in an overhanging corner and we could see trees below us in the mouth of the cave. The rope reached perfectly despite our misgivings and we found ourselves at the mouth of one of the oldest caves in the world. The others followed and we entered the cave together, completely overawed by the size and grandeur of the cavern. It was 200 feet long, 140 feet wide and the top of the dome which forms its roof was 150 feet above us. Several tunnels radiated from it to end in rock falls or small windows in the east face overlooking the jungle far below. A small spring ran through one gallery to a handy slab in the mouth of one of these openings and here we made our kitchen.

We arrive at our 'kitchen', make camp and cook a simple meal

We spent three nights in the cave. While Wilmur made a detailed survey of the whole cave system with Carlos, David and I circumnavigated the whole mountain via the horizontal fault that ran around the mountain at the height of the caves.

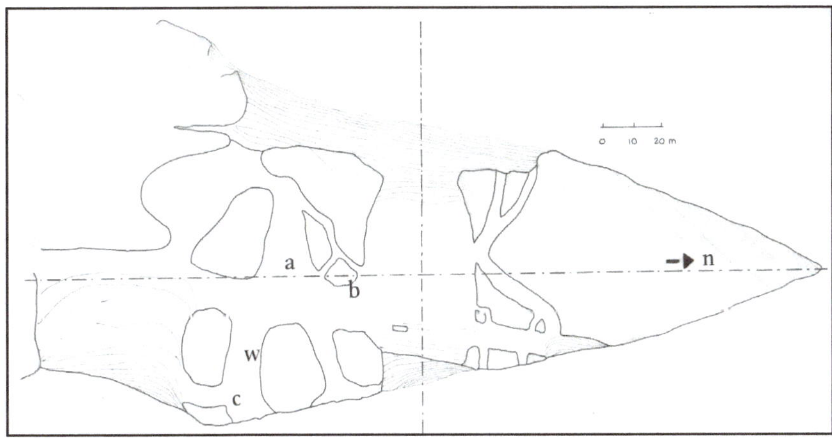

Survey of the cave by Wilmur Perez and Carlos Reyes. We slept at point ***b****, our kitchen was at point* ***c*** *and our water supply, the pool shown below, was at point* ***W****.*

Reflections in the pool, our supply of drinking water

Views from the cave, and circumnavigating the mountain

Climbing the chasm that separates the main tower from the 'tail' of the Autana. In the upper half we climbed the aluminium laddar left by Charles Brewer and David Nott.

On the third day we completed the ridge to the summit and on the fourth began the descent. Night caught us abseiling down the last overhanging 300ft wall and we stumbled back to base camp by the meagre light of our only pocket torch. Daniel and the Makiritare were waiting for us and, mistaking our jubilant whoops for attacking Indians, gave us a daunting reception with machetes in hand.

Daniel was there waiting for us. He had tried to follow us and had jumared up the ropes we had left until they ran out. He and the Makiritare had eaten all the food. So jokingly the Indians threated to eat the young Yanomami they had with them. He slipped away with a spear and a while later we heard him shouting that he had trapped a babar, a small caiman, in a rock pool.

It was this that sustained us the next three days as we paddled and drifted back down river, the outboard motor having failed to start.

Carlos Reyes with summit knoll in the background

Wilmur Perez on summit with Cerro Wichuj in background

Juan in the prow paddling us back in the rain after the outbaord motor failed

Notes

As well as our climb described here in 1974, there have been various ascents of the Autana. Charles Brewer, David Nott and Robert Madden descended to the caves after landing on the summit from a helicopter in 1971. There were ascents by Daniel Genoud, Wilmur Perez and Carlos Reyes in 1978 from either side of the mountain direct to the caves and an ascent by an English expedition of Leo Houlding, Jason Pickles and Sean Leary who made a movie called 'Autana - first ascent in the lost world'.

https://www.youtube.com/watch?v=WzBaPd3OxmM

Jaime "Jimmy" Marull flew through the cave in a microlight in 1988.

http://www.dailymotion.com/video/x99kf2_jimmy-marull-autana-flight_shortfilms

Amazonas, the largest state in Venezuela, it covers one fifth of the country a total surface area of 176,899 km2 but is home to less than 1% of the country's total population many of them indigenous people from a number of tribes. (142,000 in 2007).

The Autana was declared a national monument in 1978. One hundred and thirty-two species of plants are now known from the summit, of which seven are new to science, four new to Venezuela, one new to the flora of the Guayana Highland, and sixteen newly recorded for the flora of Territorio Federal Amazonas. (Steyermark, 1974)

References

Boletín de la Sociedad Venezolana de Espeleología 7 (14): 129-145.

Zambrano-Martínez, S., R. Lazo y C. Kalinhoff. 2004. Monumento Natural Cerro Autana. En: Rodríguez, J. P., R. Lazo, L.A. Solórzano y F. Rojas-Suárez (eds.) Cartografía Digital Básica de las Áreas Naturales Protegidas de Venezuela: Parques Nacionales. http://ecosig.ivic.ve (Consultada el 25/07/06).

Brewer-Carías, C. 1976. Cuevas del Cerro Autana. Natura (Sociedad de Ciencias Naturales La Salle) 58: 33-47.

Colveé, P. 1973. Espelología Física: Cueva en Cuarcitas en el Cerro Autana, Territorio Federal Amazonas. Boletín de la Sociedad Venezolana de Espeleología 4(1): 5-13.

Dunsterville, G.C.K. 1975. Orquídeas de la Cima del Cerro Autana. Acta Botánica Venezuelica 10 (1-4): 251-262.

Martini, J. y F. Urbani. 1982. Noticiero Espeleológico: Sveita, Nuevo Mineral de la Cueva del Cerro Autana (Am. 11, Venezuela). Boletín de la Sociedad Venezolana de Espeleología 10 (19): 210-211.

Martini, J. y F. Urbani. 1985. Sveita, un Nuevo Mineral de la Cueva del Cerro Autana (Am. 11). Teritorio Federal Amazonas. Boletín de la Sociedad Venezolana de Espeleología (21): 13-16.

SVE (Sociedad Venezolana de Espeleología). 1976a. Catastro Espeleológico de Venezuela: Am. 11 – Cueva del Cerro Autana. Boletín de la Sociedad Venezolana de Espeleología 7 (13): 81-85.

SVE (Sociedad Venezolana de Espeleología). 1976b. Noticiero Espeleológico: Ascenso al Cerro Autana. Boletín de la Sociedad Venezolana de Espeleología 7 (13): 114-116.

Steyermark, J. 1974. The summit vegetation of Cerro Autana. Biotropica 6: 7-13.

Steyermark, J. 1975. Informe sobre la Flora del Cerro Autana. Acta Botánica Venezuelica 10: 219-233.

Julian A. Steyermark I BIOTROPICA 6(1): 7-13 1974 Instituto Botanico, Ministerio de Agricultura y Cria, Caracas, Venezuela

Urbani, F. 1976. Espeleología Física: Ópalo, Calcedonia y Calcita en la The Summit Vegetation of Cerro Autana Cueva del Cerro Autana (Am. 11), Territorio Federal Amazonas, Venezuela.

Araguaney, Tabebuia chrysantha, *Venezuela's National Tree*

www.ingramcontent.com/pod-product-compliance
Lightning Source LLC
LaVergne TN
LVHW052302100826
845147LV00001B/118

* 9 7 8 1 9 1 2 4 6 0 0 1 4 *